Chase The Wind

Chase The Wind
A Book Of Poetry

Sherman Kennon

authorHOUSE®

AuthorHouse™
1663 Liberty Drive
Bloomington, IN 47403
www.authorhouse.com
Phone: 1-800-839-8640

Published by AuthorHouse   07/13/2012

ISBN: 978-1-4772-2941-5 (sc)
ISBN: 978-1-4772-2942-2 (e)

Library of Congress Control Number: 2012912723

Contents

Glow

You are as a flower
that glows beautifully in the sun.
You shimmer as pure gold
nothing less than a treasure to behold.
Your smile has the power
to warm the coldest soul.
Your love and compassion
are of an ocean stretching for unending miles.
You are as the purest diamond!
You surpass shining!
You forever glow!

Captivated

I'm captivated at the mere
mention of your name,
fascinated by the beauty of your smile.
I desire your presence
whenever you're away,
I frown upon the thought
of you being gone to stay.
I dream of the day
that you truly know the depths
of my love,
the day you realize
its strength is powered
from God above.
Never doubt,
just always know
the depths of my love.

Sherman Kennon

Best

You deserve the best,
so never settle for less.
Always look too progress,
excelling above the rest.
Stay strong in faith,
ready for any test.
Be second to none,
always striving to be the best.

Born to the Streets

A child was born to the streets of the ghetto.
Extremely hard times seemed
all he would seem to ever know.
It seemed no matter how hard he tried
the streets continued to knock him down.
Every day, his mommy would tell him,
"Baby, don't let these streets defeat you!"
In return, he would tell her,
"Mommy I'm gonna make you proud of me!"
Each time he would suffer a blow
from the mean streets,
he would hang on the words,
"Mommy I'm gonna make you proud of me."
As time went on,
survival allowed this child
to grow into a man.

Hence growing into a man
and surviving the streets
ultimately meant
he made his mommy proud of him.
In life, we will be knocked down,
but we gotta get up.
We should all wanna make somebody
proud of us.

Chance

Upon my arrival,
I'm greeted with respect.
During my stay
I felt utter neglect.
At my departure,
I'm questioned why the short visit.
My attempt to return
left cause for concern.
My opportunity to speak
was interrupted by
others' desire for my silence.
But again I will
have my chance.

Born

Some are born to lead.
Others are destined to follow.
No matter the path,
we are all born
to be great.

Change

Is it possible to change things,
or do I allow things
to change me?
Will I even try
or just let things be?
There are things that need changing,
so do I sit back and wait,
or do I let change begin
with me?

Sherman Kennon

Dark Is the Night

Dark is the night,
then day return the light.
Beautiful are the flowers,
looking too the clouds
for rendering of needed showers.
Still is the water
conveying rest for its inhabitant.
Calm are the stars
glowing too beautify the sky.
Peaceful is a land
that fear not the greed of man.
Happy will be the day
when love conquer all
and hate suffer
the eternal fall.

Flow

By the water that flow calmly,
a breeze that blow
thinking or maybe wondering
where for does it go?
Beneath hold life abundant
of many perhaps never seen
but too of his great creation.
So one will believe
if belief is in what is seen
or maybe not seen,
true it is there
as true as time will pass,
never too stand still.
Each moment embrace
or more so cherish.
As gentle the wind blows,
wrap yourself
within its flow.

Chase the Wind

I chase the wind
and get lost in the clouds.
I'm sweep into darkness
in my search for the light.
I see the future
but get caught up in the past.
I strive for first.
It sure beats coming in last.
Still I chase the wind
and float as a gentle breeze
up among the stars
then descending
as a bird down amidst the trees.
Still I chase the wind,
gradually gaining
yet never gaining.
Still forever,
I chase the wind.

Focus

I chase the stars
and wonder where they lead.
I follow the wind
in search of the calm that follows.
I sometimes seek shelter from the rain.
Other times I relish the moisture that it brings.
I enjoy the cold of winter
but find myself longing for the heat of summer.
I gaze at the moon,
and I'm fascinated by the stars.
I love being free.
I cringe at the thought of being confined.
My mind sometimes wonders,
but my focus remains clear.

Sherman Kennon

Greatness

*It was assumed that greatness
could not be achieved
but then it was questioned,
how can that be determined
if one has yet to pursue it?*

In This Room

All alone in this room,
thinking about you
and all we've been through.
The days are long and never-ending.
I constantly wonder
if you'll be coming back.
I cannot change what happened in the past,
but I can make our future
brighter and happier.
Together, we can make it last forever.
When you have weighed
all options,
considered all reasons to stay away,
it is here that I will be waiting

Sherman Kennon

and trusting that you will return
to the only man
who will love you more
than you ever thought
you could be loved.

I Wondered

I wondered if I'd see you again.
If so, would I know what to say?
I never knew I would miss you so much,
never knew I could love so deep.
The hours have been long,
the days never-ending.
Now that you're here
and I'm looking into your eyes,
I need the words to be perfect,
words that will blow your mind.
I must choose my words wisely,
making sure they are correct and true.
I'll start with love and end with love.
What comes in between,
I must still think on.

Come Together

Day doesn't just turn to night.
Nor does night just turn to day.
There is a transformation,
a blending or coming together.
We as a people
must do the same.
We must come together.
Apart, we are more vulnerable
to the evils that exist,
but together,
we are mighty and strong.
Come together.

Dawn

As dawn sets on another day,
I reflect back and contemplate
on the day's journey.
On this day,
I traveled many a mile,
at the very least.
To some, hopefully,
I brought a smile.
If I accomplish this,
perhaps the journey
is worthwhile.

Live

Live, laugh, and love,
for precious
are the days
that we are blessed to see
and be part of.
Live, laugh, and love.
Enjoy all gifts
given from God above.

Love Somebody

This world was created
from love,
so love is of this world.
We are of this world,
making us full
of love.
Love somebody!

My Baby

Your smile can change my mood
from bad to good.
For my survival,
I need you just as I need food.
It seemed a lifetime that I desired
to have my soul mate.
Now that I have you,
I realize that it was fate.
Now my dreams are our dreams,
but I've multiplied them
ten thousand times more.
Together, we are strong,
and we continue to grow
as time go on.
You're such a beautiful lady.
You'll always be my baby.

Lovely Night

It's such a lovely night.
The wind is calm,
and the stars so bright.
You are more beautiful
than ever before.
If my heart skipped a beat before,
tonight, it skips two, three,
or even more.
It's such a lovely night.

My Love

Oh, my love,

how I long for your touch,

how I long for the whisper of your sensuous voice.

I'm at total loss when you are not near.

My life is empty without you hear.

Oh, my love, when will you return?

I have strength of patience, but the separation

causes me great concern.

Oh, my love, it is

only you for me,

and I can be the only one for you.

New Day

Every day is a new day
with new possibilities and opportunities.
We can't change
what happened yesterday,
but we can
impact what happens today.

Of My Concern

Heat flowed from the room as fire.
Anger had taken over the calm
that once dwell.
I ask to talk,
you scream to be left alone.
I turn to walk away,
you imply I have no time.
I return to listen,
you insist it's not my concern.
I assure you it is
my concern,
and of your problem
I'm eager to learn.
Again, I ask what's wrong,
you reply nothing
and tell me to just move on.
So again, I walk away,
but you then ask me to stay.
Again I ask,
"What is wrong?"

Nothing Else

Indeed it is love,
for nothing else can be so pure,
nothing brings such happiness,
of nothing else have I felt so sure.
There are things I can do without,
things that leave much doubt,
but what I am sure of
is the essence of your love.
My heart I open,
allowing my love to connect with yours.
We join together
and trust that our love lasts forever.
Indeed it is love,
for nothing else can be so pure.

Onward

The terrain is rough,
the hills are high,
but giving up means I'll surely die.
So I continue on.
Of my path still unsure.
I cross over the rocks,
wade through the rushing water.
I climb the steep cliffs,
fight through the rain-filled storms.
Miles have I, too, travel.
Easy it's sure not to be,
but giving up will surely
mean the end for me.

React

This world can sometimes be bitterly cold,
grasping at the very fibers of our soul.
The evils exist—that's a fact,
but we gotta stop and think
before we react!

Search

I struggle through the dark
in search of the light.
I sometimes want to give up
but realize
that winning means
continuing to fight.
Often I'm considered wrong
even when I've proven myself right,
sometimes told to
just give up and accept the loss,
but victory is very much in my sight.

So Proud

Born a child grown into a man,
always believing in yourself
with the determined attitude of,
"Yes, I can!"
You've done what has been asked of you,
been humble as God desires you to be.
We're all so very proud of you.
I'm amazed at the brightness
the future holds for you.
Goals are unlimited long as you.
Do the things you're supposed to.
As you close one chapter and begin on another,
there are things that will be left behind,
but there are things you must take with you,
the two most important being
God and family.

You are now primed for many of life's situations,
but beware of future temptations.
Stay strong, be true,
and always remember we love you!
Congratulations on your graduation!

Son of a Queen

Born of a Queen,
learned to be a man from a King.
raised to be a star,
for doing right never to stray far.
Raised to strive for first
but be gracious
if I find myself second best.
My roots run deep
and are spread wide.
My blood is of the richest form.
Expected of me are great things,
so I must meet or exceed
these things
to be worthy of being the son
of a King and a Queen!

Sherman Kennon

The Beginning

In the end, will we seek the beginning?
In the beginning, do we fear the end?
On this journey of life,
will we travel with faith
or blindly wander,
using caution with every step?
Will we respect what is right
or disrespect and do what is wrong?
Will we settle for the less that is given,
or will we strive for more that is available?

Speak Out

I turn on the news
and hear of nothing but violence.
Perhaps it's time we speak out
and end this code of silence.
Some fight over things
that have no real meaning.
Others kill, even though
they know that's not God's will.
Stop the violence
and let the love increase.
Today and every day,
let there be peace!

Sherman Kennon

This Dance

May I have this dance
that I might hold you tight?
I wish for this song
to last forever
that I might hold you through the night.
I've always enjoyed this song
but never as much as now.
I softly sing along
as a harmonizing whisper
gently in your ear.
I can't remember you more beautiful
than you are right now,
my love.
May I have this dance
that I might hold you through
the night?

Time will change

Time will change
as also will the days.
Many things will change, and from that we find good,
but if your
heart is pure
and your love is true,
these things have no reason
for change.

The Light

You turned to the left,
but your destination was to the right.
You searched for the stars,
then realized
it was day and not night.
You went in search of peace,
but everyone you encountered
had a desire to fight.
Many questioned
why you continued moving forward.
I can only imagine
it was because
at the end of the tunnel,
you could see the light.

Still a Lie

A bird is still a bird
even if it can no longer fly.
A fish is still a fish
even if it loses its ability to swim.
A dog is still a dog
even if it never barks.
A tree is still a tree
even if it has lost all of its leaves.
A lie is still a lie
even if it's disguised
as the truth.

Sherman Kennon

To Fail

To fail is to have never tried.
If I fail but have tried,
then I can still raise my head
with pride.
With success or with failure,
I can hold my head high,
for in my heart,
I know I did try.

Success

Success is given to very few.
For most of us
to obtain it we must
seek and conquer it.
My destiny must be success
because I refuse to fail.
I look to God for strength,
and with it, I prevail.

Transformation

As the day transforms into the night,
the dark will give way to the light.
As fall and winter
give way to
spring and summer,
the heat will transition back to the cold.
The world is filled with peace and love,
yet the world is full
of evil and hate.
I realize that there are many negatives
I'll face along my path,
but I can't be derailed
on my search for all that is good.

Trust Him

In the mist of the storm
when you're tired confused
and your body is worn,
when friends have turned and walked away,
when it seems you can't make it through another day.
When darkness never seems
to allow the light to shine,
when it seems you're running out of time,
when you've done all you can
and feel you can do no more,
remember that God is able,
trust Him!

Sherman Kennon

The Truth

You say that you love me,
but you treat me so cruel.
You say I'm your friend,
but you don't want others to know.
You say you're not prejudice,
but you frown upon my race.
You say we're all equal
but consider yourself better than me.
You fall on your knees and pray
then witness injustice
but choose to look away.
You speak holy each and every Sunday
but spread hate every other day.
You judge me, though
you know it's not your right.
Instead of getting along,
you'd rather fuss and fight.
Yet through it all,
you say that you love me.

Truth

If it's easy, will it be taken for granted?
If it's hard, will it be given up on?
If unsure, will we ask for truth?
If truth cannot be found,
will we rely on a lie?
If a lie is all we hear,
will we give up on knowing the truth?
If we give up on the truth,
will we forever live a lie?

Ultimate Flight

On a late night,
confident that my mind was right
for a journey yet traveled,
so ultimately, I took flight.
My pace was swift,
my determination unsurpassed.
Not only was it my first
but also to be my last.
From the start, it was obvious
the journey would be hard,
but never could I lose focus,
never could I let down my guard.
For the journey,
my body I had to train,
also needed was for me to have
a strong, determined brain.
Whether crossing the rugged mountains

or sailing along the placid waters,

I had to be ready.

I had to prevail.

I had to win.

I had to succeed.

I would not fail.

Unyielding

I grasp for things I cannot see.
I long for power I cannot have.
I wait for that which never come.
I call out to that which
does not exist.
I lay in hope of rest.
I strive in spite of rejection.
I hunger for more of what is good.
I strive for peace and love.
I fight resistance from every direction.
I'm told things will never change,
but I'm determined
to make a difference.

Why

Why do some hate
when it's so easy to love?
Hate derives from evil,
but love
is from God above.

Your Day

This day we set aside
and call it yours,
but for all you do and have done,
you deserve so much more.
I trust that you know all that you mean to me.
I believe you're everything
God desires a woman to be.
You're strong of courage,
faith, support, and of course, love.
You're truly a blessing sent from above.
Your worth cannot be captured
in just one day,
but we set it aside in celebration
and trust that the memories
never fade away.
For this day, tomorrow,
and every day thereafter.
Happy Mother's Day!

Understanding

With understanding,
we will find love.
With love,
there will be unity.
With unity,
there can be peace.

To Night

As day transform to night,
Soon, dark give way to light.
The seasons will ultimately change,
as it is true
nothing remains the same.

This Love

Today is a special day,
for this day, we celebrate our love.
Yesterday was also special,
for we celebrated our love.
It is a love that no other can claim.
There are none who can understand its depths,
none who would realize its true power.
Tomorrow, we will celebrate our love,
and every day thereafter,
we will celebrate this love,
for it is a love that has no end.

The Stars

The stars so bright bringing life
to the dark skies of night.
I reach because they appear so close,
but reality reminds me that they're so far away.
This same distance is that of your touch
for the farther I reach,
the more distant you become.
Voices in my head urge me to leave you alone,
but the desire of my heart
reminds me
that I'm not that strong.
I fear that you are as a star,
appearing so close
that I feel I can touch you
but actually being so far away
that I never will.

Thank You

I've been selfish
not to do your perfect will.
Good as you've been,
it seems the very least I can do.
You've been there through the highs,
been my strength through the lows.
It's easy to see why
you're my all and all.
So I lift you up
and give you all the praise,
not just this day
but every day thereafter.
You are all power,
mighty and strong.
For all you've done,
all you are doing,
and all you will do,
thank you!

Sherman Kennon

About the Author

Sherman L. Kennon works in the automotive industry in Lincoln, Alabama. This is his second book of poetry. His first book is titled *My Thoughts*, which was published in 2010. Sherman has been writing poetry for many years, and he writes on many different topics. He currently resides in Oxford, Alabama, with wife, Jessica, and he continues to write poetry.

About the Book

*C*hase the Wind is an inspirational book of poetry. It touches on many different topics—God, life situations, and the beauty of life—and of course the book speaks of love and its unlimited power. *Chase the Wind* has poems that uplift, inspire, and motivate.